Outdoor mural, Majuro Atoll.

Majuro

Essays from an Atoll

By Floyd K. Takeuchi and Olivier Koning

Store sign, Majuro Atoll.

Contents

Two boys and their chickens, Laura, Majuro Atoll.

Joys of Discovery

TRAVEL AT ITS BEST is about the joy of discovery. The joy of pulling back the curtain of a hotel room window and seeing a placid lagoon shimmering in the early light of day. The joy of turning left instead of right, and finding oneself in a small shop whose owner becomes a new friend. The joy of taking a seat in a restaurant that isn't in any of the guidebooks, and eating a memorable meal.

For those fortunate enough to travel to the Marshall Islands, there is always a sense of discovery. It isn't easy to get to the Marshall Islands; the intrepid traveler must choose to get to the collection of atolls and small islands in the Central Pacific that make up the Republic of the Marshall Islands. There's none of the "let's take that train instead" decision-making that one can do on a continent.

But the traveler who finds himself or herself in the Marshalls will often be rewarded for the effort. This is travel for the adventurous, not for those who preen or insist upon being pampered. It is an experience for those who wish to learn. Indeed, those who travel to these atolls to learn about others will find that they leave learning more about themselves.

These essays and photographs represent our journey to Majuro, capital of the Marshall Islands. We traveled to Majuro for the Marshall Islands Visitors Authority. Our brief was to develop a fresh take on life in these islands. For nearly two weeks, Olivier Koning and I traveled over the atoll, sailed across its lovely lagoon, and spent an exciting day aboard the sport fishing boat the XXXX in the waters off Majuro and neighboring Arno Atoll.

Our travel, and thus this book, was made possible thanks to the Marshall Islands Visitors Authority's board of directors, General Manager Dolores deBrum-Kattil and Marketing/Research Officer Emelyn Simon. We must also give special thanks to Bill Weza, the veteran hotelier who runs the Marshall Islands Resort, Ramsey and Colette Reimers of the Hotel Robert Reimers (and a host of other Majuro enterprises), and Continental Micronesia for their generous and significant support.

Many individuals, from handicraft entrepreneurs and artisans to college presidents and administrators to canoe builders to church pastors, priests and congregations, also welcomed us as if we were long-lost friends. And one of the joys of traveling to the Marshalls is that after one trip, you will indeed be considered an old friend when you return, as you will.

FLOYD K. TAKEUCHI
HONOLULU, HAWAII

Eneko Island kitchen-dining room and bungalow complex.

How to find Paradise

Story by Floyd K. Takeuchi
Photographs by Olivier Koning and Floyd K. Takeuchi

Is there anyone who doesn't have a private island fantasy? Someplace where you can forget your problems, be surrounded by quiet beauty, unplug from the rest of the world.

I'm thinking about my private island fantasy as our skiff skims across the lagoon of Majuro Atoll, close in on the lee of small, jewel-like islands. They slip by one after another, covered by coconut palms, thick and emerald green, nestled in a white sand setting, surrounded by turquoise water so clear individual coral heads and darting fish are visible from 40-feet above.

Majuro, the capital of the Republic of the Marshall Islands in the Central Pacific, has 53 islands and islets. Most of them along the northern-edge of the atoll are deserted, though here and there a small house is visible through the palms. But clans claim all of these islands, no matter how small, and in traditional times, even these islets would serve a purpose. Marshallese would paddle their canoes here to gather coconuts and breadfruit, or perhaps to hunt birds, certainly to catch fish in the surrounding waters, and sometimes to just get away from nosey neighbors or hectoring spouses.

Today, for those fortunate enough to venture to Majuro, which is about 2,300 miles south-southwest of Honolulu, a number of the atoll's islands have been converted into retreats. Living accommodations range from eco-rudimentary to posh, but no matter the choice the experience is the same – a sense of tranquility that comes from basing your schedule on the tides, the wind and the sun.

My retreat is Eneko, an island that is a micro-version of paradise. Our boat driver gently nudges our skiff onto a brilliant white sand beach facing the lagoon, and we jump into cool, knee-deep water so clear it seems to disappear. Just ahead are a bungalow and a separate meetinghouse with its own kitchen and bar. The thick grass lawn gives way to a forest of towering coconut palms, whose fronds rustle in the steady trade winds.

The sound of the wind through the fronds is a constant companion on Eneko, natural white noise. Not that there is a lot of competing noise to block out on this island. The only other steady sounds are the Pacific pounding against an ocean-side fringing reef – a low-pitched rumble filtered by the thick coconut groves – and the gentle hiss of lagoon waves washing up on a beach that's only 30 feet from the porch of the bungalow.

This retreat is the vision of Ramsey Reimers, a Marshallese business executive whose family plays the leading role in the country's nascent visitor industry. Ramsey first concentrated on the local market – yes, it is possible to get harried and stressed working on an atoll where there are no secrets. Eneko's first buildings included a barbecue and picnic shelter and fresh-water showers, perfect for a weekend family picnic.

But Ramsey was keen on appealing to the country's small visitor market, which he already served with a popular downtown hotel, the Hotel Robert Reimers, named for his late father. Why not give the visiting trader or international official a chance to spend a night or two in an outer atoll environment, but be a convenient and safe 25-minute boat ride away?

So Ramsey built a screened kitchen-dining room building and a bungalow. The sleeping accommodations are simple but comfortable. One bedroom has a private bathroom. Two other bedrooms share a bathroom. The bungalow can sleep six on beds, though the use of traditional woven sleeping mats could easily up that number.

Known for his visionary ideas, Ramsey also decided to power Eneko primarily with a small solar-based system. There's enough power to run lights, and a small pump that provides fresh water (rainwater in catchments) for showers. A small gas generator also provides back-up power.

Eneko is for those who enjoy the lack of distractions. There are no televisions or radios in the bungalow. There is no Internet connectivity. There is no schedule of planned activities or a concierge. And while you can use your mobile phone on Eneko – get a local telephone number and SIM card from the national telecommunications authority first – what's the point?

What there is on Eneko can keep you busy enough. There is fantastic snorkeling in crystal-clear water. Fields of colorful coral are an easy kick or two from shore. Even the novice diver (rent snorkel gear at the Shoreline dive shop at the departure dock) can swim with colorful tangs and angelfish, which dart among the coral heads.

There's also a floating dock for those energetic enough to swim from the beach to the deck attached to pontoons. And there are single and double kayaks available for those who would rather paddle

Lagoon beach, Eneko Island.

13

their time away.

Beachcombers will find a large beach along the lagoon side, and a rugged coral coast on the north-facing ocean side. At low tide, you can walk toward the reef on the ocean side but use caution – parts of the reef shelf can be razor sharp, and the tide can come in quickly.

But mostly, Eneko, like the other get-away islands in the Majuro Atoll, is a convenient and comfortable retreat from reality. There's nothing to worry about on the island. The Reimers' hotel sends out the boat with freshly made meals three times a day. And we traveled to Eneko with a cooler filled with cold drinks, snacks and fruit. The only other people on Eneko are the family that takes care of the island, who also ensure that guests have a trouble-free stay.

On our first night on Eneko, sitting on the lagoon beach under a sky thick with bright stars, the only sounds were the gentle beat of lagoon waves, and the ever-present rumble of the ocean rolling over the far-away reef. I thought about what constituted "reality" on an island that seemed so removed from my usual urban life.

I looked across Majuro lagoon to the far eastern edge of the atoll, where most people live, and I watched the bright lights of the capitol town twinkle in the night. And then they disappeared. Nearly every light on Majuro went dark within 15 seconds, the result, we later learned, of a power outage at the atoll's only power plant.

So there we were, sitting on a perfect beach under a clear tropical night sky. And across the lagoon, some 25,000 people, nearly half the country's resident population, was in the dark without power.

Suddenly, in the lagoon just in front of me, no more than 30 feet from shore, two beams of light in the water swept the coral heads. Two of Eneko's caretakers were spear fishing, using flashlights to attract their prey. The night would turn out to be good for fishing.

As I watched their underwater beams arc through the lagoon, with the warm glow of solar-powered lights casting soft shadows across the beach, I thought about all of the people in Majuro's urban area who were at that moment no doubt cursing the sudden dark and loss of lights, television and air conditioning.

And I thought to myself, sometimes unreality is the best reality of all.

OLIVIER KONING

Lily on Eneko Island.

Northside islands, Majuro Atoll.

OLIVIER KONING

17

First light of day over Eneko Island, with moon still in the sky.

FLOYD K. TAKEUCHI

Boat's wake, Majuro lagoon.

OLIVIER KONING

21

Canoe bow, Majuro lagoon.

Sailing into the Future

STORY BY FLOYD K. TAKEUCHI
PHOTOGRAPHS BY OLIVIER KONING

MENTIL LAIK HAS the strong, rough hands of a man who uses them to earn a living. But his calloused fingers move with surprising dexterity as he weaves fibrous coconut twine through the narrow confines of the outrigger of a miniature Marshallese sailing canoe.

Laik gently guides and tugs at the strong twine, which he made moments before from the fibers of coconut husk by rubbing them against his thigh. He's an expert at all things related to the canoes of the Marshall Islands, even on a model designed to be exhibited at the world expo in Shanghai.

At 55, Laik has been building the beautiful traditional canoes of the Marshall Islands for more than 30 years. He apprenticed on his home atoll of Ailuk with his grandfather, a master canoe builder. For the past seven years, the soft-spoken Laik has been the teacher for a score of Marshallese youth who are learning the ways of their ancestors.

He's part of a unique skills-building program that looks to the past to prepare at-risk Marshallese youth for the future. Formed in 1999, but based on work that began 10 years before to document traditional canoe-building skills that were being lost, Waan Aelon in Majel (Canoes of the Marshall Islands) is a unique example of finding value in an indigenous culture to prepare its young people to survive in a commercial world.

You would think that all things related to the sea would come naturally to young Marshallese. Their nation spreads out over the Central Pacific, just above the equator. It is comprised of 34 coral atolls and islands scattered across an ocean area of 1 million square miles. The young nation's capital, Majuro Atoll, home for Waan Aelon in Majel, is about 2,300 miles south-southwest of Honolulu.

But many of today's young Marshallese who grow up just a stone's throw from the Pacific Ocean, are disconnected from their maritime heritage.

"We've got kids who don't know how to swim," says Alson Kelen, the energetic Marshallese who is director of Waan Aelon in Majel. So swimming is among the skills that Kelen's trainers pass along to each class, which can number around 20.

Originally designed to focus solely on reviving traditional canoe-building skills, Waan Aelon in Majel today takes a broader view of training. The ancient ways of hewing the foundation of a canoe hull from a breadfruit tree is still required learning. But so too are modern carpentry skills, which can also be used to make furniture, as well as building traditionally-styled canoes protected and strengthened by fiberglass.

"Today it is about jobs. People expect to be able to get jobs when they learn skills," notes Kelen, who has been with the program from its beginning. That practical attitude is understandable at a time when, by some estimates, the nation's unemployment rate is about 30 percent. But if the practical coexists with the traditional at Waan Aelon in Majel, so too does a respect for the program's roots in Marshallese culture. Revered elders are brought in to share stories with each class, which studies for six months at the program's canoe house on Majuro.

In recent years, to the surprise of some, young women were allowed to compete along with men for a place in incoming classes. But Kelen says that while going coed was a change, it reflects an understanding of the critical role women played in the development of a canoe culture in the Marshall Islands.

Marshallese are recognized as having had some of the region's finest traditional navigators, who could steer their voyaging canoes by using the position of stars and the feel of waves. And, says Kelen, in Marshallese lore the first navigator was a woman, Litarmelu. Women also wove the sails that made Marshallese canoes some of the fastest in the Pacific.

While Waan Aelon in Majel's efforts are focused on training young people, it has also spurred a revival of Marshallese canoe building and sailing. Today, at least two regattas are held in the islands. Long-distance sailing over hundreds of miles has also been revived, using a 35-foot fiberglass-strengthened canoe to make the voyage.

Marshallese canoes are considered among the most beautiful in Oceania. Their hulls are rise gracefully at either end, and have the look of a craft designed for speed. A large outrigger attaches to the starboard side and provides stability and more "deck" space for longer voyages. But when sailing in a strong wind, an experienced sailor can ride the outrigger up 25 or 30 degrees into the air. It makes for a stunning sight, and an exciting time for those aboard the canoe.

Lashing a model canoe outrigger with sennit.

One of the benefits of having the canoe program is that visitors to Majuro can also experience first-hand what it is like to sail on a Marshallese canoe. For a reasonable fee, a hotel can arrange for Waan Aelon in Majel students to take tourists across Majuro lagoon in one of the program's canoes.

On the day that we headed out, the trade winds were blowing across the lagoon at about 10 miles per hour. Not a stiff wind, but enough to move the canoe along at about five knots. And given the slender shape of the hull of a Marshallese canoe, the speed seems much faster when you're actually sitting on an outrigger and spray is blowing up from the bow.

Anyone who has sailed aboard a Marshallese canoe will be amazed at the sophisticated technology of these graceful craft. The canoes sail remarkably close to the wind. Instead of the traditional tacking,
a crew member simply lifts the front of the sail out of the bow and places it in the stern of the hull. No leisurely tack needed; no ducking to avoid a swinging boom. The canoe immediately takes off in a different direction.

On our afternoon on the lagoon, the crew took the canoe through a maze of multi-million dollar fishing trawlers, many with helicopters secured to their decks. The ships are part of the purse seiner fishing fleet that uses Majuro as a base to chase tuna across the Marshall's huge exclusive economic zone.

I can't imagine what the crew members aboard those boats must of thought of our canoe as it zigged and zagged among the anchored behemoths. A few curious sailors at the railings looked down on our canoe as it darted around their ships.

As our canoe worked its way across the lagoon, I was reminded of what it was like in the 1950s when I was growing up on Majuro. In those days, it was common to see canoes sailing across the lagoon, or beached on the shore. They were often sailed by Marshallese coming in from the outer islands to buy goods at Majuro's trading stores.

The young men who sailed our canoe were likely the grandsons or, perhaps, the great-grandsons of those sailors of 50 years ago. While the times have changed, our crew and their passengers were connected to the past by our sleek blue-and-red canoe as it sliced through Majuro lagoon. For part of an afternoon, at least in our minds, the large fishing boats disappeared and we had the lagoon to ourselves.

Canoe bow.

Marshallese canoe, Majuro lagoon.

Sailing across Majuro lagoon.

Marshallese sailors, Majuro lagoon.

End of Mass, Assumption Catholic Church, Majuro Atoll.

Discovering the Pacific in a Church Pew

STORY BY FLOYD K. TAKEUCHI
PHOTOGRAPHS BY OLIVIER KONING AND FLOYD K. TAKEUCHI

THERE'S ONE SURE-FIRE WAY for a Pacific traveler to get to know the local community. Go to church.

No matter where you are in the Pacific, a church service will provide the outsider with an understanding of the community's culture, values and traditions. And in the islands, congregations welcome visitors as if they were long-lost relatives. This holds true regardless of where you are traveling, whether it is Suva or Saipan, Manu'a or Majuro.

On Majuro Atoll, capital of the Marshall Islands, there's no shortage of church services to attend. The mainstay denominations are the Protestant's Congregational Church and the Roman Catholic Church. But there are also a host of other Christian churches, many of which have evangelical congregations that are growing in popularity.

Pacific churches are also known for the beauty of their choirs, and that is certainly the case in the Marshall Islands. The Marshallese can be quiet and reserved with strangers, and a visitor to this atoll nation could think that the islanders are reserved in the extreme. But give the Marshallese an opportunity to sing, and they become one of the most outgoing people in the Pacific.

It is 10 a.m. on Sunday, and the congregation at the Assemblies of God church in Delab, on Majuro, is rocking. The colorfully dressed church members are standing, stomping feet and waving hands above their heads. Everyone is singing, and a band near the altar is driving a fast-tempo beat. And this is just the beginning of the Sunday service.

The service is more restrained down the road at the Roman Catholic mission's Assumption Church. There, the hymns are sung with equal fervor and beauty, but the mass doesn't include a band with electric guitars and a drummer. Still, the pews are filled with the faithful, and the service reminds the visitor that the Catholic service is both familiar and comforting, no matter the language spoken or the location of the church.

On Majuro Atoll, which is about 2,300 miles south-southwest of Honolulu, churches also play a key role in education. The Roman Catholic Church's Assumption School is one of only three U.S. accredited high schools on the atoll, which is the capital of the Marshall Islands, and the only church-affiliated school that meets U.S. education standards.

There are a host of other schools affiliated with churches throughout Majuro. In fact, the Marshall Islands has a high number of such schools, even compared to other Pacific nations, where church's also play a leading role in national and community life.

Indeed, religion is one of the dominating factors of life in the islands. Pacific Islanders are active churchgoers, and in some islands it isn't usual to have services throughout the week, and expect congregation members to attend multiple services on a Sunday. Generally, the pastors preach a more fundamental Christian theology. And there are still signs that remind one of the days on Majuro when congregations wore white to Sunday services. Today, there's a sea of color in the pews, but in many churches, men still sit on one side of the aisle and women on the other side, just as it was decades ago.

Every Pacific Island has its own strong religious traditions. On the island of Kosrae, part of the neighboring Federated States of Micronesia, some congregations used to practice public confessions during services. It made for some interesting gossip, and no doubt helped to keep church attendance up on that strongly Protestant island.

Fiji's dominant Methodist Church used to have an annual conference, whose highlight was a competition of church choirs from across that 300-island nation. I can remember my first year in Fiji, when I worked as a newspaper editor in the capital of Suva, and the joy of hearing the bus loads of choirs before they passed me on the streets. The churches would charter buses, which in those days had open sides, and the choirs would practice on their way in to Suva from the outlying villages.

The Samoas have some of the strongest church traditions in the Pacific, and in both American Samoa and independent Samoa (formerly Western Samoa), most churchgoers still wear white when they attend Sunday services. At those churches, all women wear fancy white hats and the men are usually in white jackets with a matching white lava-lava wrap.

A drive from Samoa's Faleolo International Airport into the

OLIVIER KONING

Graveyard, Majuro Atoll.

capital of Apia reminds a visitor of the power of churches in that country. It seems that every fourth or fifth structure is a church along the beautiful drive into Apia. The same is true on Majuro, where churches are commonplace along the 30-mile road that connects the community of Rita at one end of the atoll with village of Laura at the other end.

Outsiders are sometimes critical of the influence of Western missionaries in the Pacific Islands. But I've yet to meet an islander who complains about Christian traditions and values, which have been incorporated into daily lives with enthusiasm. In nearly every island across the Pacific, Christian traditions and theology mesh seamlessly into indigenous concepts of culture and values.

So it is no surprise that in the Marshall Islands, people take their religion seriously. At the Assemblies of God church on Majuro, for example, tithing by the congregation has meant the huge church is cooled by nine giant air conditioners, and the floor is covered with shiny white tiles. Some men wear coats and ties to the service, and the president of the nation is a member of the congregation. The Marshall Islands church has sent its members to meetings in the United States, where there are large expatriate Marshallese communities in Hawaii and Arkansas.

At the Roman Catholic Assumption Church, a new multi-storey classroom building for its school was built with donations. Work on the new building began before all the funds were in hand, a sign in part of the church's confidence that its parishioners would find a way to fund the completion of the building. It was indeed completed and serves the well-regarded Assumption School.

For visitors to the Marshall Islands, the Christmas holiday is the most interesting time to attend a local church service. Nearly every church goes all out during the holiday to welcome the festive season. In many Protestant churches, there's a tradition of groups of congregation members entering the service singing and energetically dancing and swaying.

Members practice long hours, and the holiday services can run for hours. Oh, did I mention the food?

FLOYD K. TAKEUCHI

Students, Assumption School, Majuro Atoll.

Sunday service, Assemblies of God Church, Majuro Atoll.

OLIVIER KONING

Singing hymns, Assemblies of God Church, Majuro Atoll.

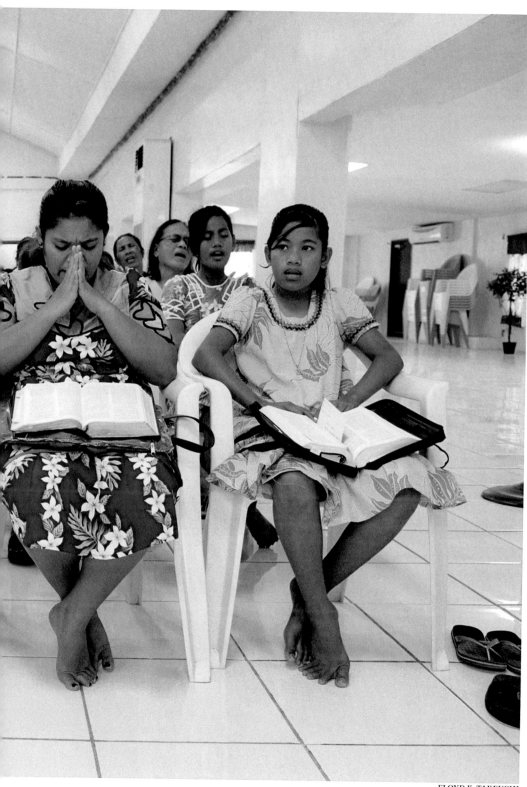

FLOYD K. TAKEUCHI

43

Protestant church, Majuro Atoll.

OLIVIER KONING

Cooked pandanus with grated coconut.

More than Coconuts and Fish

STORY BY FLOYD K. TAKEUCHI
PHOTOGRAPHS BY OLIVIER KONING

IN YEARS OF TRAVELING throughout the Pacific Islands, I've learned many important things, some of them the hard way. Appropriate cultural practices. The best hotels to stay in. When the hurricane season is above and below the equator. And how early I should get to the airport to lessen the possibility that I'll be bumped or have my suitcase go walkabout.

But nothing compares with the knowledge of the best places to eat. And, in the Pacific for those truly interested in local culture, there's a corollary: which restaurants offer the best local foods.

Here's the dirty secret about Pacific travel: in many islands, if not most, it can be hard for the visitor to find many traditional dishes on restaurant menus. Oh, the hotels in most islands will offer one or two dishes that are considered "local." But the hard core foodie may have to work extra hard to enjoy a meal comprised of farm-to-table cuisine or, perhaps more appropriately in the Pacific, farm-and-sea-to-table.

There are three exceptions, to varying degrees, to the rule in the Pacific: the Samoas, French Polynesia and Fiji. One can find a number of local dishes, such as palusami in Apia, or kokoda in Nadi, on many hotel restaurant menus.

Now add a fourth Pacific destination to the list for the epicurious traveler. It is Majuro Atoll, capital of the Marshall Islands in the Central Pacific.

It is an unlikely destination for the foodie. The young country has a nascent visitor industry, and the atoll's major hotels, while welcoming and fun to stay at, don't have classically trained chefs running white-linen restaurants. In the Marshalls, instead, one finds a small but enthusiastic restaurant scene that's finding innovative ways to incorporate atoll produce and the rich harvest of the sea in daily menus.

For a nation with 1 million square miles of ocean surrounding its 34 atolls and islands, it is no wonder that fish plays a huge role in Marshallese cuisine. The Marshall Islands was administered by Japan from 1919 until U.S. forces invaded in 1944, so it isn't surprising that

Marshallese are partial to the Japanese preparation of sashimi, thin slices of raw fish to be seasoned with a splash of soy sauce mixed with wasabi. Locals add their own touch with a squeeze or two of the calamansi citrus fruit.

The Marshall Islands has an active fishing industry – tuna loins prepared in the Marshall Islands can be found in vacuum-sealed bags sold at most Costco warehouse stores in the U.S., for example – and that means the tuna used for sashimi in Majuro restaurants is fresh, really fresh. As in just hours off the boat fresh.

Fish is also offered in a number of other preparations – sautéed, grilled, with various sauces. Tuna is usually commonly found on menus, but so too is wahoo, a particularly moist white flesh fish, and mahi-mahi

It is also possible to find on some menus fish that are found closer to shore, such as grouper. The Enra Restaurant at the Marshall Islands Resort prepares grouper in a light breaded crust, and the fish's flesh is flaky and light. The dish, and others that feature local ingredients, are the creation of Chef Jitban Jacklick, a Marshallese whose creativity makes her kitchen one of the most interesting on Majuro.

Indeed, some of the most exciting experiments in fine local cuisine are taking place at the Enra. The restaurant is known for its pandanus brulee, which uses the rich pandanus fruit to make a velvety brulee.

At the other end of town, the Tide Table Restaurant always has Marshallese dishes on the menu, such as various preparations of breadfruit. That you can also find specials, such as Mexican dishes, is an extra benefit! Owner Ramsey Reimers also offers a healthy option plate each day.

The restaurant, located in the Hotel Robert Reimers, also offers the juice of the pandanus. It is difficult to make – pandanus is a fibrous fruit and it took months of trial and error to figure out how to extract the juice from the hard "nuts" of the plant. The juice is definitely worth trying, and it is reminiscent of a citrus and guava mix. Food scientists at a U.S. university ran an analysis of the juice, and found it rich in vitamins, Reimers says.

One of the more interesting places to find hearty Marshallese food is at the unusually named DAR Coffee Corner. It is located on the ocean side of Majuro, on the backside of the atoll's post office. There's usually a buffet offered at DAR, and it's a popular place for Marshallese to buy pumpkin and rice, bwiro (preserved breadfruit) or ma kalel (breadfruit cooked in coconut milk) when in season, and

Bounty of the land and sea, Majuro Atoll.

jaibo (a Marshallese favorite that is flour cooked with coconut milk and a little sweetening and is served like soup).

Remarkably, Majuro has also developed an active farming sector. This is hard to believe, given the poor soil found on most atolls, which are primarily coral. But on Majuro's western end, in an area called Laura, a hangover from the U.S. Navy's time, local farmers are now growing cherry tomatoes, cucumbers and other produce. It's the result of an innovative small-scale agricultural program developed by Taiwan. The Taiwan agricultural extension center at Laura has helped farmers identify crops that can thrive in Laura's loamy soil.

The result has been a small boom in locally grown produce, which is also making its way onto restaurant menus. This is a big deal. Before the advent of an active farming sector on Majuro, all fresh produce was brought in from the U.S. West Coast by airfreight. Local farmers can't provide all the produce consumed on Majuro, but the local market has enthusiastically received their vegetables. Indeed, no other island nation or territory in the Western Pacific produces as much produce as is grown by farmers on Majuro.

There are other choices on Majuro for the traveler looking for interesting places to eat. The country has a growing Chinese population and there are two particularly popular Chinese restaurants, Monica's Restaurant in town and Won Hai Shen near the commercial dock. There's even a small health food restaurant, run by the Diabetes Wellness Center, that's located near the International Convention Center, next to the main government buildings.

But perhaps nothing compares with the experience of being invited by a Marshallese family to join them on a picnic. I was fortunate enough to be invited by Senator Tony deBrum, a Member of Parliament and a friend of many years, to join his family for a Sunday picnic. We traveled by boat from a dock at his home to a small island at the northern end of the atoll that's owned by his family.

In a cooking shed, the women prepared a large fire using dried coconut husks. It's the Marshallese version of mesquite, producing hot even heat and smoke, and the result on marinated chicken is sublime. Simple side dishes – a salad and rice cooked in rich coconut cream – rounded out the meal. The family also broke out chilled, husked coconuts to drink. To top off the meal, the nuts were cracked open and we scooped out the soft, sweet coconut meat.

Sitting in the shade, watching the fire's smoke rise into the coconut fronds, it was hard to remember when I have had a more satisfying meal.

Sunday picnic, Majuro Atoll.

Young coconuts, Majuro Atoll.

Breadfruit, Majuro Atoll.

Pandanus fruit, Eneko Island, Majuro Atoll.

Marshallese dishes at the Enra Restaurant, Marshall Islands Resort.

Lunch featuring local dishes at the Enra Restaurant, Marshall Islands Resort.

Trolling lure, Majuro Atoll.

A Good Day: Reeling in the Bounty

STORY BY FLOYD K. TAKEUCHI
PHOTOS BY OLIVIER KONING

CAPTAIN BEN REIMERS is having a good day. His boat, the 36-foot XXXX, is making its way along the southwestern coast of Arno Atoll in the Marshall Islands. We're outside the fringing reef, but the sun is so bright and the air so clear, it looks as if we could reach out and touch the coconut trees that cover Arno's islets.

The XXXX, a converted steel-hulled U.S. Navy launch that's named for an Australian beer, has five trolling lines in the water. Behind his wrap-around dark glasses, Reimers, a veteran sports fishing skipper, keeps an eye on the boat's instruments, the reef and the horizon, always looking for the tell-tale sign of fish – a flock of birds.

But then we get a hit! One of the big gold Penn International X reels begins to screech, and Ronnie Reimers, Ben's uncle, moves quickly to one of the rods. Wilson and Nakol, our fishing crew, are also in action, bringing in the other lines and unhooking the pole from its guideline. Ben throttles back, keeping enough power to control the boat, and all eyes are on the water some 30 yards behind the XXXX.

With an experienced fisherman's calm demeanor, Ronnie works the reel as a 15-pound mahi-mahi puts up a terrific fight. These aren't only good eating fish, the mahi-mahi is also a fighter, and this one is no exception. But in a few minutes, Ronnie has the iridescent colored fish aboard the stern deck and the fish is dropped into an iced cooler. The lures are checked, and lines are dropped back into the Pacific. Ben turns up the throttles, and we resume our run for more fish. It's that kind of day.

In traditional times, of course, fishing wasn't a sport for Marshall Islanders. It sustained them, providing the protein to balance the limited starches and fruits that could be found on their coral islets. And fortunately for those Marshallese, their watery nation, comprised of 34 atolls and islands just above the equator in the Central Pacific, has some of the richest fishing grounds in the region. The fleet of Asian and American deep-sea fishing boats, and their mother ships, that today use the Majuro Atoll lagoon as a home port, confirms that fact. Majuro is the capital of the Republic of the Marshall Islands, and is about 2,300 miles south-southwest of Honolulu.

Today, the Marshall Islands is recognized as having some of the finest big game fishing in the Pacific, bar none. There are two major fishing tournaments each year, one in July and the big tourney, the All Micronesia, in September. The All Mike's record catch is a 794-pound marlin, snagged by a crew from Pohnpei Island in the neighboring Federated States of Micronesia. That marlin was caught just off Majuro Atoll, near the international airport.

Aboard the XXXX today, however, marlins remain an elusive catch. But Ronnie, assisted by Wilson and Nakol, are plenty busy. Once we clear Majuro's lagoon and head into the open ocean for the 45-minute trip to Arno, the fishing crew is on the alert. It isn't long before we get our first strike.

It's a 10-pound mahi-mahi, small but still a good fighter. About 10 minutes later, another strike and another small mahi-mahi. Ben, our experienced captain, then tells the crew to pull in the lines. We're running with a school of dolphins, which dart around and ahead of us as we head toward Arno Atoll.

The dolphins peel off as we get within sight of Arno, which has three lagoons instead of the usual one found on atolls. Ben's eyes are darting over the ocean, looking for the best course to begin some serious trolling.

He knows what he's doing because a few minutes later, there's a third strike, this time a 15-pound mahi-mahi. And it is a real fighter. A few minutes later, our fourth strike, another mahi-mahi. And then 15 minutes later, Ronnie brings in the first of the day's many wahoo, this one a 12-pounder.

For the next two hours, the XXXX will have seven more strikes, wahoo and mahi-mahi. The boys are busy on the stern, reeling in the fish, resetting lines, scanning the horizon for the tell-tale clouds of black birds following schools of fish. When we see the birds, Ben kicks up the throttle and the XXXX's inboard Diesel engine roars to life.

Early in the afternoon, just shy of four hours on the water and about three miles off Arno Atoll, the big Penn reel starts to scream. All eyes turn toward the ocean, as we see the tip of the big fishing rod dip sharply. Ronnie moves quickly to the fighting chair, and straps himself in and the sets the rod and reel into the mount, and then snaps closed the rod's security line. Given the strain on the line,

Yellow-fin tuna, caught near Arno Atoll, Marshall Islands.

and the fight being put up by the catch, we know this is a big fish.

For nearly 10 minutes, Ronnie works the reel, yelling instructions to Wilson and Nakol. Ben looks over his shoulder as he expertly maneuvers the big boat to give his uncle the best position to fight the fish. And then the fish is close enough to the side of the XXXX for us to see it glisten in the water, still fighting, darting to port and starboard in a desperate bid to loosen the lure.

But the combined experience of Ronnie in the fighting chair and Ben at the boat's wheel proves too much. With a gaff in hand, Wilson hooks the fish and strains to bring it aboard the XXXX. That's when we see that the catch is a 60-pound yellow-fin tuna, a big beauty.

Ben decides it is time to head back to Majuro, though on the way he continues to scan the horizon and the XXXX heads toward any flock of birds that's circling a patch of ocean. We will have four more strikes on the way back to Majuro. Ronnie will land two of the fish, a mahi-mahi and a wahoo, but two other fish will slip the lure. The last fish brought aboard is a 10-pound wahoo, caught near the channel that will lead us back into the calm waters of Majuro lagoon.

Ronnie has landed close to 275 pounds of fish on our day on the ocean. The prize, of course, is the 60-pound yellow fin. But the iced hold full of mahi-mahi and wahoo is nothing to complain about, and the boys are rightly pleased with the day's haul.

As we near Majuro's Shoreline dock, just next to the Reimers' family hotel, Ben eases back on the XXXX's throttle and the engine's roar turns into a rumble.

"It was a good day," says Ben. "It would have been good to catch a marlin. But it was a good day."

We later heard that Ben was able to sell most of the fish to the family's Hotel Robert Reimers, which is named for his late grandfather. No doubt Ben kept some for himself, and Ronnie, Wilson and Nakol also went home with fresh fish that day.

Ben offers us some of the haul, too, but with only a small hotel refrigerator and no kitchen, it would be a waste of good mahi-mahi or wahoo. Instead, we have great memories of a beautiful day on the ocean, and a bountiful harvest from the sea. As Ben said, it was a good day.

The XXXX tied up behind inflatable dinghies at the Shoreline Dock,
Majuro Atoll.

Reeling in the catch near Arno Atoll, Marshall Islands.

Hosing down a just-caught yellow-fin tuna.

Catch from bottom fishing in Majuro lagoon.

Preparing trolling lines off Arno Atoll, Marshall Islands.

Hand of master weaver Patsy Herman, and dried pandanus leaves.

Woven Artistry:
The Pacific's Finest Handicrafts

STORY BY FLOYD K. TAKEUCHI
PHOTOGRAPHS BY OLIVIER KONING

A CORAL ATOLL seems an unlikely place to showcase the power of using local resources. At first glance, the low-lying islets that comprise an atoll, none rising more than five- or six-feet above sea level, have few natural resources beyond sand, coconut and breadfruit trees, and the bounty of the sea.

But in the Marshall Islands, a watery nation in the Central Pacific made up of 34 atolls and islands with 1 million square miles of ocean, women have developed a tradition of producing the finest handicraft in the Pacific using local resources. The claim is not an exaggeration.

In American Samoa in 2008, more than 2,000 islanders from 23 Pacific Islands nations and territories, the best artisans and dancers, participated in the 10th Festival of Pacific Arts. The festival, held every four years, is the Olympics of Pacific culture and crafts. The Marshall Islands had a small booth showcasing and selling its traditional handicrafts – exquisitely made purses, mats, wall hangings and jewelry fashioned from tightly woven pandanus and indigenous shells.

The audience of some of the best Oceanic artists cleaned out the booth in less than two days, and the Marshallese organizer said she could have sold another shipping container's worth of handicraft. A member of the Samoan delegation, no slouches when it comes to traditional crafts, told me the Marshallese handicraft was the finest she'd ever seen.

On Majuro Atoll, capital of the Marshall Islands, Patsy Herman is recognized as one of the young nation's finest weavers. Her specialty is jaki, woven mats that have served many purposes over the centuries. When Western explorers first stumbled across the Marshall Islands, mats were worn as clothing and also used for sleeping. Some of the best examples of those magnificent jaki can be found in the collection of the Bishop Museum in Honolulu.

Today, jaki are primarily decorative or used as hangings. I have a 3-foot by 3-foot "baby mat" that was given to my parents when I was born on Majuro in the early 1950s. It is a lovely piece – seven distinct patterns using two colors in a mat made of tightly woven pandanus leaves stripped to no more than one-quarter inch wide. The weave is so fine that the mat feels like starched cloth rather than something made from the leaves of a hardy plant that thrives in the harsh climate along beaches.

But rather than have the mat left unprotected, I've had it framed in archival materials. It's a shame to not be able to touch the mat, but the thought of such an important piece of family history being exposed to the elements or insects is too scary to consider.

As is often the case with weavers in the Marshall Islands, Patsy learned the art by watching her mother. She started to work with the pandanus leaves when she was in the fourth grade. Today, at 44, she's teaching her two daughters how to weave.

"She thinks they'll become weavers, too," says Maria Kabua Fowler, a Marshallese of high traditional rank who is a recognized cultural authority and has been a driving force to train more young women to become weavers, particularly of jaki.

Most Marshallese handicraft is made from the pandanus leaf. The leaves, which have serrated edges, are dried and then pounded to soften them. The leaves are then rolled into wheel shapes, from which weavers cut the leaves into thin strips. The finest weavers will be able to work with strips that are about one-quarter inch wide, and using just their hands, weave mats, hats and purses with incredibly fine weaves.

Patsy shows us a hat that she's making for an official at the U.S. Embassy on Majuro. She had taken his head measurement the day before. Today, the hat is nearly done, the weave as fine as any fancy hat produced in Central or South America.

One of the most popular handicraft items is what the Marshallese call a wut, a woven head lei that depicts intricate flowers and other plant life. Some flowers are colored; others are the brilliant white that characterizes so much of the finest Marshallese woven handicraft.

A few years ago, few women were seen in Majuro wearing the woven wut. Today, it is a commonplace fashion accessory, just as stunning as shell necklaces, sometimes with matching shell earrings, and bracelets. Fans are also a popular and useful handicraft item.

But perhaps the best-known, and most prized fashion piece is the so-called Kili Bag. It is to the Pacific what the Hermes Kelly bag is to French couture. No exaggeration – a few years back, I saw a Kili Bag in a special display at one of the toniest department stores in Honolulu. I recognized its distinctive shape, and when I went closer to look at the bag, I saw its price tag, $1,500. An extremely fine large Kili Bag on

Master weaver Patsy Herman displays a hat after one day of weaving.

Majuro will go for much less, usually around $45 in most stores.

Like so much in the Marshall Islands, the Kili Bag is a product of beauty that arose out of necessity. The people who live on Kili Island are originally from Bikini Atoll, site of U.S. atomic tests during the 1940s and 1950s. Unlike Bikini, which has a large lagoon and many islets that can grow food, Kili is a barren island with no natural harbor. In the 1950s, women decided they needed to do something to bring more money to their then struggling community. So they organized themselves around something they were skilled at, weaving handicraft, and developed a woman's purse of exquisite simplicity and beauty. The Kili Bag is woven of brilliant white pandanus leaves, has a single rectangular compartment with an attached form fitting flip-top lid. The two handles form a graceful U.

Today, most Kili Bags are woven on Arno Atoll, which is near Majuro. No matter. The bags are still stunning.

But in the same spirit that led the women of Kili, 50 some years ago, to develop their distinctive purse, today's Marshallese weavers are in the midst of a creative bloom. The number of new designs, both of handicraft products and designs of existing bags and implements, is stunning.

Marshallese weavers are particularly good at drawing creative inspiration from new forms and fashions, as well as from the past. Recent exhibits that brought old jaki, some dating to the 1800s, to Majuro from the Bishop Museum collection, stunned many weavers, who had never seen the old designs. Soon, they were incorporating some of the patterns into contemporary handicrafts.

A visitor to Majuro has a number of fine handicraft shops from which to choose excellent work. There are five main shops on the island, as well as handicraft centers in other stores, and each carries variations of hats, women's purses, intricate wall hangings, trivets and coasters, and jewelry.

A new item that's become extremely popular is single woven flowers. The smaller ones, some of which are colored with dye, are worn over the ears of women; the larger ones are used in arrangements.

And it is possible to order a jaki, the traditional woven mat. It is an individual work of art, and it takes most weavers around two months to make a mat that one might have worn in traditional times. Prices for a mat that size run about $200. Given how much work goes into weaving a jaki, these stunning mats are among the best value handicraft that a visitor can buy in the Marshall Islands.

Marshallese handbags.

Lily models Marshallese handicraft jewelry and accessories.

Zoya wears a woven wut, or head lei, with flower, jewelry and fan.

Handicraft artisan uses cowrie shells to make Marshallese jewelry.

Woven Marshallese wall hangings on display in a handicraft shop, Majuro Atoll.

Lily on the beach, Majuro Atoll.

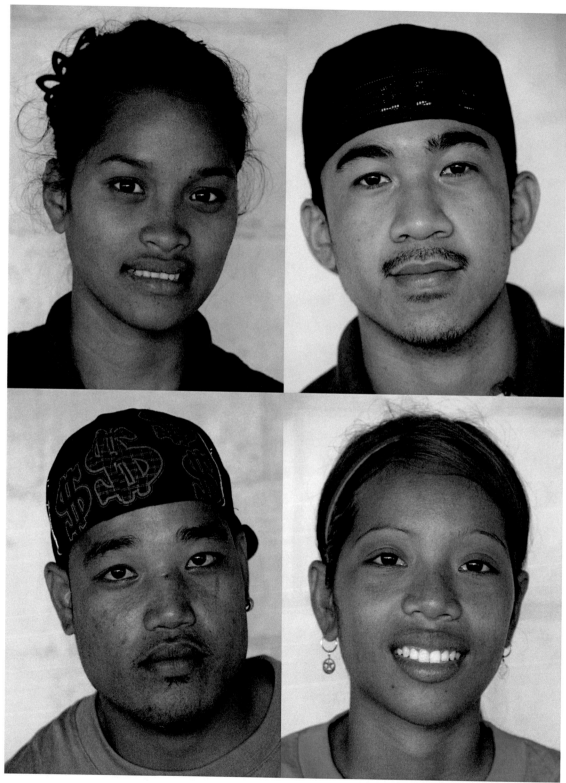

Portraits of a People

IT IS EASY FOR OUTSIDERS to think of Pacific Islanders as being one people. They all live on islands, some large, some small. They all have somewhat similar traditions, based in many cases on a seafaring past, a reliance on limited resources, and cultures that place a premium on control of the land.

But the reality is that saying "Pacific Islanders" are similar is akin to saying all Europeans are the same, or that Americans are one people. It isn't true, and the convenience of broad brushing a people and culture masks the remarkable ethnic and cultural diversity that can be found on nearly every island in Oceania.

That's certainly the case in the Marshall Islands. Despite being isolated in the Central Pacific with a national population of fewer than 70,000, the peoples of these lovely atolls and coral islands are remarkably diverse. You can see it in their faces – beauty, without a doubt, but also their history of voyaging to other parts of the vast Pacific, and the influx of foreigners who first began traveling to this remote group hundreds of years ago.

Over the centuries, Spain, Germany, Japan and the United States laid claim to the Marshall Islanders. All the while, of course, the Marshall Islanders knew these were their islands and often went about their business. But the waves of foreigners left a genetic imprint in the Marshall Islands, a history that's evident in faces as well as family names, which are as diverse as Kabua, Anjain, Luther, deBrum, Reimers, Bing and Chutaro. Today's reality is that there is remarkable diversity in a people who are blessed to live on atolls and islands of stunning beauty. That reality is evident in the faces of today's Marshall Islanders.

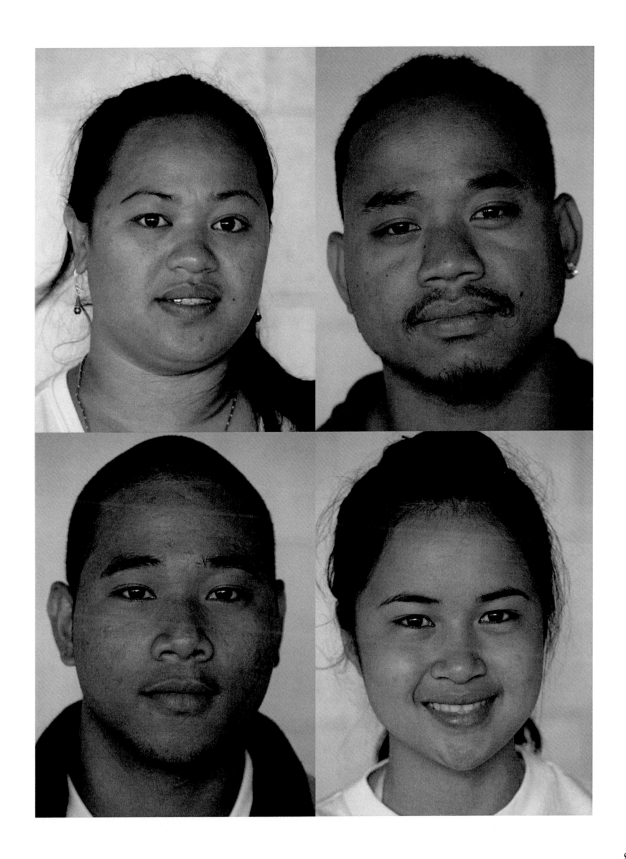

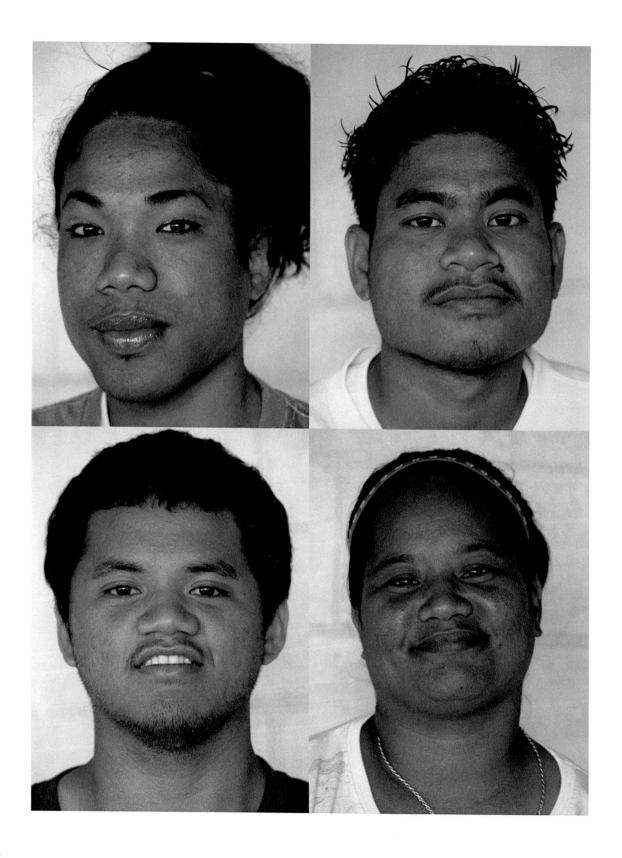

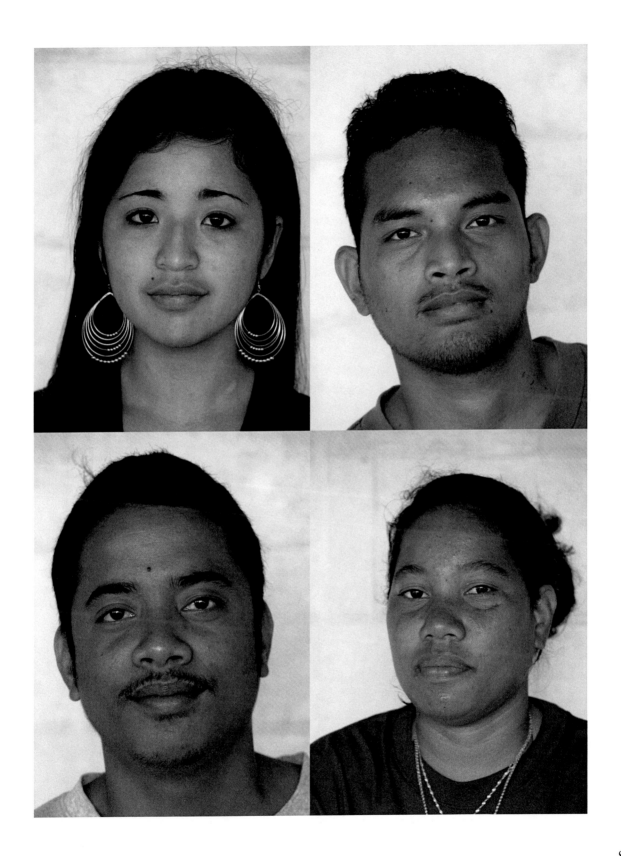

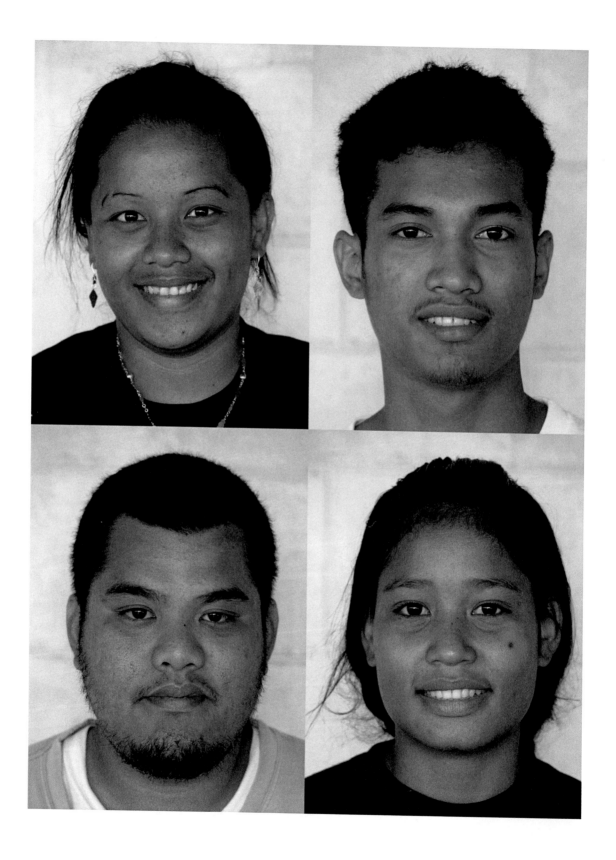

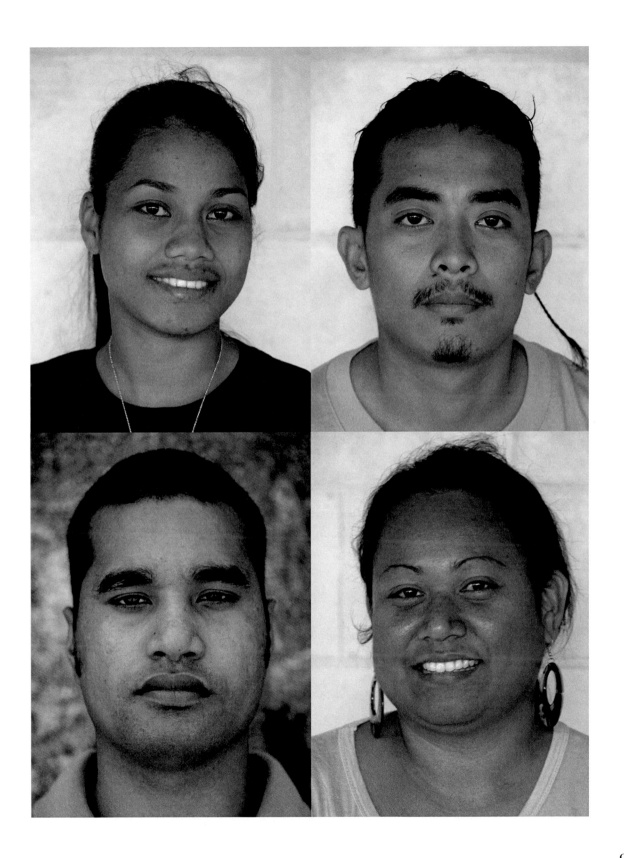

The Authors

OLIVIER KONING

FLOYD K. TAKEUCHI

Floyd K. Takeuchi is a writer-photographer who specializes in the Pacific Islands, which have been his literal and emotional home for five decades. He has traveled to nearly every corner of Oceania, and worked as a journalist in the islands. He's also been a reporter, editor, radio and television anchor and publisher in Hawaii and Japan, and once became confused and spent two years as a senior staffer for a Member of the U.S. House of Representatives in Washington, D.C. Floyd was born and raised in the Marshall Islands.

FLOYD K. TAKEUCHI

OLIVIER KONING

Olivier Koning has made the Hawaiian Islands his home for 25 years. Born and raised in France in a multi-cultural family, he has completed photographic assignments in Hawaii, the Samoas, and Marshall Islands, as well as shot in Southeast Asia and Europe. Olivier's work has appeared in publications as diverse as Wallpaper, Honolulu Magazine, Polynesia Magazine, Pacific Magazine, The Kahala and the publications of Story Worldwide. Olivier's photography in Samoa for Polynesia Magazine won a major national design award in the United States.

OLIVIER KONING

Pandanus leaves, Eneko Island, Majuro Atoll.

ISBN: 978-0-615-39388-9

Library of Congress Catalog Card Number: 2010934546
Floyd K. Takeuchi and Olivier Koning
Majuro: Essays from an Atoll

For more information on visiting the Marshall Islands:
Marshall Islands Visitors Authority: www.visitmarshallislands.com
Eneko Island: http://www.rreinc.com/hotel-beaches.htm
Continental Airlines: www.continental.com

For more information on the authors:
Floyd K. Takeuchi: www.floydtakeuchi.com
Olivier Koning: www.olivierkoning.com

Cover Photos: Olivier Koning
Book Design: Malcolm Mekaru

Majuro Atoll.

OLIVIER KONING

Mural inside a taxi stand, Majuro Atoll.

OLIVIER KONING

28904418R00058